M000202045

25 DAYS OF ANTICIPATION

JESUS...THE FULFILLMENT OF
EVERY HEART'S LONGING

LOVE WORTH FINDING MINISTRIES

innovo
PUBLISHING

Published by Innovo Publishing, LLC
www.innovopublishing.com
1-888-546-2111

Providing Full-Service Publishing Services for Christian Authors, Artists & Ministries: Hardbacks, Paperbacks, eBooks, Audiobooks, Music, Screenplays, and On-line & Physical Courses

25 Days of Anticipation: Jesus . . . the Fulfillment of Every Heart's Longing

ISBN: 978-1-61314-779-5

Cover Design: Jeff Hatcher
Interior Design: Innovo Publishing, LLC

Printed in the United States of America
U.S. Printing History
First Edition: 2021

Introduction

Thanks for stopping by during the Christmas rush!

Whether you are a Christian or someone who wants to know more about Jesus, we're glad you're here.

This is a mini Bible study—a daily selection of Bible readings with two paragraphs of devotional thought and a question or two to ponder.

We're going to be looking at prophecies regarding the Messiah alongside passages documenting the fulfillment of those prophecies in Jesus Christ.

We hope this book greatly enhances your Christmas advent season as you contemplate the babe in the Manger as the Creator, the fulfillment of prophecy from Genesis through Revelation, and the answer to the longing in every soul.

So, grab your Bible and a cup of warm cocoa.

Sit with us by the fire a while and warm your heart!

DECEMBER 1

Jesus—God of Creation

READING HIS STORY

Prophecy Proclaimed

In the beginning God created the heavens and the earth. —Genesis 1:1

Then God said, "Let Us make man in Our image, according to Our likeness; let them have dominion over the fish of the sea, over the birds of the air, and over the cattle, over all the earth and over every creeping thing that creeps on the earth." —Genesis 1:26

Have you talked to a 2-year-old lately? Even young children know to use the word "I" or "me" when talking about themselves alone. Here our Creator God uses the plural "Us." The plural pronoun expresses His unique nature as God the Father in total harmony with His unique nature as God the Son and likewise God the Holy Spirit. "In the beginning, God" refers to the Trinity.

Prophecy Fulfilled

In the beginning was the Word, and the Word was with God, and the Word was God. He was in the beginning with God. All things were made through Him, and without Him nothing was made that was made. —John 1:1-3

We may have difficulty grasping the concept of God as three-in-one, but John makes it clear in his opening statements that Jesus is the very God of creation. John refers to Jesus as the Word and states: "the Word was with God, and the Word was God." He goes on to say that at creation, "nothing was made" without Jesus. The Apostle Paul puts it this way in Colossians 1:16-17, "All things were created through Him and for Him."

WRITING YOUR STORY

Have you thanked the Triune God for creating you?

You can speak to God as Father, Son, and Holy Spirit, thanking Him for giving you life.

What does it mean to you that you were created "for" Jesus?

DECEMBER 2

Jesus—Victorious from the Beginning

READING HIS STORY

Prophecy Proclaimed

And I will put enmity between you and the woman, and between your seed and her Seed; He shall bruise your head, and you shall bruise His heel. —Genesis 3:15

Jesus' birth and His victory over Satan are prophesied here in the very first book of the Old Testament. After Eve, and then Adam, both succumb to temptation, God tells Satan, "I will put enmity between you and the woman, and between your seed and her Seed." Throughout the Bible, the word "seed" refers to the offspring of a male, but here God speaks of the "Seed of the woman." Seed is capitalized because it refers to God Himself in the person of Jesus Christ—a prophecy of the Virgin Birth.

Prophecy Fulfilled

> But when the fullness of the time had come, God sent forth His Son, born of a woman, born under the law... —Galatians 4:4

Jesus was "born of a woman," but not of a man, having instead the sinless genetic make-up of God Himself. He was born "under the law" into a world under judgment. In the sacrifice of His sinless life, He was the only one who could redeem us from the law of sin and death and offer us grace. As we accept His grace, we are born again, not "of the will of man, but of God" (John 1:13), with our Heavenly Father's spiritual DNA.

WRITING YOUR STORY

Have you accepted the offer of God's grace?

If not, what is holding you back?

If so, in what ways are you different now that you have your Father's spiritual DNA?

DECEMBER 3

Jesus—Born of a Virgin

READING HIS STORY

Prophecy Proclaimed

Therefore the Lord Himself will give you a sign:
Behold, the virgin shall conceive and bear a Son,
and shall call His name Immanuel. —Isaiah 7:14

Many people struggle to accept the Virgin Birth because it is so obviously a miracle, but the Virgin Birth, prophesied some 700 years before its fulfillment in Bethlehem, is fundamental to the Christian faith.

Prophecy Fulfilled

Now the birth of Jesus Christ was as follows: After His mother Mary was betrothed to Joseph, before they came together, she was found with child of the Holy Spirit. Then Joseph her husband, being a just man, and not wanting to make her a public example, was minded to put her away secretly. But while he thought about these things, behold, an angel of the Lord appeared to him in a dream, saying, "Joseph, son of David, do not be afraid to take to you Mary your wife, for that which is conceived in her is of the Holy Spirit. And she will bring forth a Son, and you shall call His name Jesus, for He will save His people from their sins." So all this was done that it might be fulfilled which was spoken by the Lord through the prophet, saying: "Behold, the virgin shall be with child, and bear a Son, and they shall call His name Immanuel," which is translated, "God with us." Then Joseph, being aroused from sleep, did as the angel of the Lord commanded him and took to him his wife, and did not know her till she had brought forth her firstborn Son. And he called His name **Jesus**. —Matthew 1:18-25

Without the Virgin Birth, Mary is a harlot, Joseph is a fool, and Jesus is a mere son of Adam. Without the Virgin Birth, there is no one qualified as the sinless substitute and therefore no salvation. Without the Virgin Birth, we are all stuck as we are with no way forward. By repeating the words of the prophecy and providing a detailed account of events, Matthew emphasizes the reason for the Virgin Birth—Immanuel, God with us, sinless from birth, will "save His people from their sins."

WRITING YOUR STORY

Have you struggled to accept the Virgin Birth because it is not part of our normal human experience?

In what ways do you think our increasing reverence for scientific data has hampered our capacity to grasp Divine concepts, believe in miracles, and grow in faith?

In what ways has scientific discovery strengthened your faith?

DECEMBER 4

Jesus—Passover Lamb

READING HIS STORY

Prophecy Proclaimed

"But you, Bethlehem Ephrathah, though you are little among the thousands of Judah, yet out of you shall come forth to Me the One to be Ruler in Israel, whose goings forth are from of old, from everlasting." —Micah 5:2

When Herod the king heard this, he was troubled, and all Jerusalem with him. And when he had gathered all the chief priests and scribes of the people together, he inquired of them where the Christ was to be born. So they said to him, "In Bethlehem of Judea, for thus it is written by the prophet: 'But you, Bethlehem, in the land of Judah,

> are not the least among the rulers of Judah; for out of you shall come a Ruler who will shepherd My people Israel.' " —Matthew 2:3-6

We know that Micah is referencing a Person of the Trinity because His "goings forth are from old, from everlasting." It was understood by Old Testament scholars, including the chief priests and scribes of Jesus' day, that the Messiah would have His earthly beginnings in Bethlehem.

Prophecy Fulfilled

> Joseph also went up from Galilee, out of the city of Nazareth, into Judea, to the city of David, which is called Bethlehem, because he was of the house and lineage of David, to be registered with Mary, his betrothed wife, who was with child. So it was, that while they were there, the days were completed for her to be delivered. And she brought forth her firstborn Son, and wrapped Him in swaddling cloths, and laid Him in a manger, because there was no room for them in the inn. —Luke 2:4-7

Bethlehem is a little village five and a half miles south of Jerusalem. We might never have heard of it had not Mary's little Lamb been born there. How fitting! For centuries the

Jewish priests had been raising a special breed of lambs in Bethlehem, the best of which, the unblemished, were sacrificed during the Passover to atone for sin. Here in Luke, the perfect sacrifice, as prophesied, was born in a Bethlehem stable and laid in an animal trough. He would "atone" for all sin for all time. He would make it possible for us to be "at one" with God.

WRITING YOUR STORY

Do you get the warm fuzzies when viewing a Christmas nativity display? How does knowing that Jesus was raised to be a sacrificial lamb impact your view of the manger?

DECEMBER 5

Jesus—Light of the World

READING HIS STORY

Prophecy Proclaimed

The people who walked in darkness have seen a great light; those who dwelt in the land of the shadow of death, upon them a light has shined. —Isaiah 9:2

"Where is He who has been born King of the Jews? For we have seen His star in the East and have come to worship Him." —Matthew 2:2

Christmas and light are so intertwined in our culture we could hardly have one without the other. Even those who don't connect Christ with Christmas derive physical and emotional warmth from glowing candles, crackling fires,

23

star-lit trees, and colorful neighborhood light displays. The wise men from the East followed a great light to Bethlehem because they were driven by a desire for something deeper, a spiritual fire that could not be quenched. They followed a lesser light, a star, hundreds of miles by night in search of the Great Light that has dawned on "those who dwelt in the land of the shadow of death."

Prophecy Fulfilled

And the light shines in the darkness, and the darkness did not comprehend it. —John 1:5

Then Jesus spoke to them again, saying, "I am the light of the world. He who follows Me shall not walk in darkness, but have the light of life." —John 8:12

Of course we all dwell in that shadowed land...until we meet the One who extinguishes darkness. Jesus told those who were following Him—both those who already saw Him as Lord and those who were just beginning to squint in recognition—"I am the light of the world. He who follows Me shall not walk in darkness, but have the light of life." Once we fully open our eyes, He shows us a spiritual spectrum we did not know existed. We can walk anywhere He sends us. Christ at our sides, we have the eternal assurance that the Light of the World makes darkness disappear.

WRITING YOUR STORY

Should we be content with the twinkling trappings of Christmas when the Light of the World desires our fellowship? Write about what it would mean for you to walk in the light of His presence this holiday season.

DECEMBER 6

Jesus—King, Priest & Sacrifice

READING HIS STORY

Prophecy Proclaimed

And when they had come into the house, they saw the young Child with Mary His mother, and fell down and worshiped Him. And when they had opened their treasures, they presented gifts to Him: gold, frankincense, and myrrh. —Matthew 2:11

Gold, frankincense, and myrrh, the gifts brought to Jesus by the wise men from the East, were standard gifts to honor a king in the ancient world. Many biblical scholars suggest that gold—Earth's most precious metal—recognized

Jesus as King of Kings, frankincense—an aromatic resin—symbolized His priestly role, and myrrh—a costly fragrant oil—prefigured His death and embalming. One wonders what Mary pondered in her heart regarding these gifts.

Prophecy Fulfilled

And when Jesus was in Bethany at the house of Simon the leper, a woman came to Him having an alabaster flask of very costly fragrant oil, and she poured it on His head as He sat at the table. But when His disciples saw it, they were indignant, saying, "Why this waste? For this fragrant oil might have been sold for much and given to the poor." But when Jesus was aware of it, He said to them, "Why do you trouble the woman? For she has done a good work for Me. For you have the poor with you always, but Me you do not have always. For in pouring this fragrant oil on My body, she did it for My burial. Assuredly, I say to you, wherever this gospel is preached in the whole world, what this woman has done will also be told as a memorial to her." —Matthew 26:6-13

The gold was certainly a prophetic gift. Even Pilate, in sanctioning Jesus' death, recognized Jesus as King of the Jews in John 19:1, 2 and 19-22. Revelation states that

He is King of Kings and Lord of Lords. In Exodus 30:34-38, Moses is told to make a fragrant blend of spices (including frankincense) to be placed in front of the Ark of the Covenant. God tells him, "You shall not make any for yourselves, according to its composition. It shall be to you holy for the LORD." Just before Jesus is arrested, Matthew 26:6-13 records the story of a woman breaking an alabaster jar and pouring a costly oil on Jesus, who says of her, "in pouring this fragrant oil on My body, she did it for My burial."

WRITING YOUR STORY

Obviously the wise men from the East put a great deal of thought into their gifts. What will you bring to Jesus this advent season?

DECEMBER 7

Jesus—Hunted by Herod

READING HIS STORY

Prophecy Proclaimed

Thus says the LORD: "A voice was heard in Ramah, lamentation and bitter weeping, Rachel weeping for her children, refusing to be comforted for her children, because they are no more." —Jeremiah 31:15

Here, Rachel represents Jewish women weeping for their children. As the special love of Jacob, Rachel is considered the matriarch of all Israel. Jeremiah is speaking about God's faithfulness in two circumstances. God will preserve a remnant of Israel (Rachel's children) despite the nation's exile into captivity, and He will preserve a remnant that will populate Heaven despite Herod's attempts to kill the Messiah who will save His people from their sins.

Prophecy Fulfilled

Then Herod, when he saw that he was deceived by the wise men, was exceedingly angry; and he sent forth and put to death all the male children who were in Bethlehem and in all its districts, from two years old and under, according to the time which he had determined from the wise men. Then was fulfilled what was spoken by Jeremiah the prophet, saying: "A voice was heard in Ramah, lamentation, weeping, and great mourning, Rachel weeping for her children, refusing to be comforted, because they are no more." —Matthew 2:16-18

As a baby, Jesus lived in Bethlehem with His parents. Jesus may have been about two years old when Joseph was warned in a dream to take his family to Egypt to escape the wrath of Herod who, "put to death all the male children who were in Bethlehem and in all its districts, from two years old and under." In telling this story, Matthew connects the "massacre of the innocents" to prophecy. The account also foreshadows Jesus' death at Calvary.

WRITING YOUR STORY

Moses was rescued as a baby and grew up to free his people from slavery to Egypt. Jesus was rescued as a baby and grew up to free His people from slavery to sin. What other Bible stories point to the great story of redemption? Have you been rescued by God? From what? For what purpose?

DECEMBER 8

Jesus—Waymaker

READING HIS STORY

Prophecy Proclaimed

The voice of one crying in the wilderness: "Prepare the way of the LORD; make straight in the desert a highway for our God. Every valley shall be exalted and every mountain and hill brought low; the crooked places shall be made straight and the rough places smooth; the glory of the LORD shall be revealed, and all flesh shall see it together; for the mouth of the LORD has spoken." —Isaiah 40:3-5

In those days John the Baptist came preaching in the wilderness of Judea, and saying, "Repent, for the kingdom of heaven is at hand!" For this is he who was spoken of by the prophet Isaiah, saying: "The voice of one crying in the wilderness: 'Prepare the way of the LORD; make His paths straight.' " —Matthew 3:1-3

In Isaiah, God is speaking comfort to His people. Someone is coming who will "prepare the way of the LORD." Old Testament priests and scribes took Isaiah at his word, believing that, at the proper time, a great prophet would call God's people to repent and prepare them to meet the Messiah. When John the Baptist actually appears on the scene, however, the religious leaders—the Pharisees and Sadducees—consider themselves above the message of the wilderness prophet. Their hearts remain unprepared for Jesus.

Prophecy Fulfilled

And he went into all the region around the Jordan, preaching a baptism of repentance for the remission of sins, as it is written in the book of the words of Isaiah the prophet, saying: "The voice of one crying in the wilderness: 'Prepare the way of the LORD; make His paths straight. Every valley shall be filled and every mountain and hill brought low; the crooked places shall be made straight and the rough ways smooth; and all flesh shall see the salvation of God.' " —Luke 3:3-6

Most of us think of John the Baptist as preparing the way for the Messiah's earthly ministry some 2,000 years ago. While accurate, the view is incomplete. John asked people then and, through Scripture, asks us now, to repent—turn from sin, do an about-face—and look Jesus in the eyes. Jesus is our Waymaker. He makes the crooked places in our lives straight. He makes our rough ways smooth. Through Him, we see the "salvation of God."

WRITING YOUR STORY

Have you ever discounted sound spiritual advice from someone who looked different—someone with the equivalent of camel-hair clothing and a locust-and-honey diet? From what sins do you need to turn away? In what ways do you need to "prepare the way of the LORD" in your life?

DECEMBER 9

Jesus—Good News

READING HIS STORY

Prophecy Proclaimed

"The Spirit of the Lord God is upon Me, because the LORD has anointed Me to preach good tidings to the poor; He has sent Me to heal the brokenhearted, to proclaim liberty to the captives, and the opening of the prison to those who are bound; to proclaim the acceptable year of the LORD, and the day of vengeance of our God; to comfort all who mourn..." —Isaiah 61:1-2

The heading for the 61st chapter of the book of Isaiah in one Biblical version is "The Year of the Lord's Favor." Another version titles the chapter, "The Good News of Salvation." Both speak to the fuller meaning Jesus provided for us when He read Isaiah 61:1-2 as the opening passage for His earthly ministry.

Prophecy Fulfilled

And He was handed the book of the prophet Isaiah. And when He had opened the book, He found the place where it was written: "The Spirit of the LORD is upon Me, because He has anointed Me to preach the gospel to the poor; He has sent Me to heal the brokenhearted, to proclaim liberty to the captives and recovery of sight to the blind, to set at liberty those who are oppressed; to proclaim the acceptable year of the LORD." Then He closed the book, and gave it back to the attendant and sat down. And the eyes of all who were in the synagogue were fixed on Him. And He began to say to them, "Today this Scripture is fulfilled in your hearing." —Luke 4:17-21

When Jesus said, "Today this Scripture is fulfilled in your hearing," He declared Himself the Good News. "I, Jesus," He said in effect, "come to usher in the true jubilee. I come to preach the Gospel to the poor, to open the eyes of the blind to God's plan, to heal the broken-hearted, and to set sin's prisoners free." His audience was, at first, spellbound by His claim to Divine activity. Upon reflection, His hearers questioned His words because, as the son of Joseph the carpenter, Jesus was too familiar to them to possess such greatness.

WRITING YOUR STORY

Has Jesus become too familiar to us? After so many Sunday school lessons, do we think we know all we need to know about His mission? Does He still command the respect He deserves? Write your response to His opening sermon in Luke.

DECEMBER 10

Jesus—Eternal Treasure

READING HIS STORY

Prophecy Proclaimed

Why do the nations rage, and the people plot a vain thing? The kings of the earth set themselves, and the rulers take counsel together, against the LORD and against His Anointed? ..."The LORD has said to Me, 'You are My Son, today I have begotten You. Ask of Me, and I will give You the nations for Your inheritance, and the ends of the earth for Your possession.' " Now therefore, be wise, O kings; be instructed, you judges of the earth. Serve the LORD with fear, and rejoice with trembling. Kiss the Son. ...Blessed are all those who put their trust in Him. —Psalm 2:1-2, 7-8, 10-12

A thousand years before Christ's earthly life, God talks here about the Messiah's triumph over "kings of the earth" and rulers who "take counsel against the LORD and against His Anointed." People have opposed their Creator throughout history. Some continue their opposition throughout eternity. But Jesus, with humility and suffering, wins all those who put their trust in Him. God the Father promises to give Jesus, "the nations for Your inheritance." Beloved, you're what He came here for! He wants you for His inheritance.

Prophecy Fulfilled

And the Word became flesh and dwelt among us, and we beheld His glory, the glory as of the only begotten of the Father, full of grace and truth. —John 1:14

For God so loved the world that He gave His only begotten Son, that whoever believes in Him should not perish but have everlasting life. —John 3:16

Because Jesus "became flesh and dwelt among us," lived a sinless life, and died in our place, we can be born again as sons and daughters in the family of God. At that moment, Jesus becomes our inheritance just as we are His!

WRITING YOUR STORY

Whether you know Jesus or you're still searching, how does it make you feel that your Creator wants you for His inheritance?

DECEMBER 11

Jesus—Good Teacher

READING HIS STORY

Prophecy Proclaimed

I will open my mouth in a parable; I will utter dark sayings of old, which we have heard and known, and our fathers have told us. We will not hide them from their children, telling to the generation to come the praises of the LORD, and His strength and His wonderful works that He has done. —Psalm 78:2-4

Because He cares about us and our children, God reminds us from Genesis onward to "give ear" to His law and to tell "the generation to come the praises of the LORD, and His strength and the wonderful works that He has done." Just as little children benefit when they listen and obey the

47

rules of a good parent, we profit from attending to God's teaching.

Prophecy Fulfilled

> All these things Jesus spoke to the multitude in parables; and without a parable He did not speak to them, that it might be fulfilled which was spoken by the prophet, saying: "I will open My mouth in parables; I will utter things kept secret from the foundation of the world." —Matthew 13:34-35

God's teaching must be understood spiritually. The great majority of the people in Jesus' day were not interested in God's truth. They heard the earthly stories in the parables but missed the heavenly meaning. Oh the joy for those who desired spiritual truth! He eagerly satisfied their appetites. They experienced what God meant when He said through Isaiah, "Listen carefully to Me, and eat what is good and let your soul delight itself in abundance" (Isaiah 55:1-2), and what Jesus said to them directly, "Blessed are those who hunger and thirst for righteousness, for they shall be filled" (Matthew 5:6).

WRITING YOUR STORY

Are you hungry for Truth? Write out a prayer asking the
Good Teacher to open your ears and give you understanding
as you read the Bible.

DECEMBER 12

Jesus—Living Water

READING HIS STORY

Prophecy Proclaimed

Ho! Everyone who thirsts, come to the waters;
and you who have no money, come, buy and eat.
Yes, come, buy wine and milk without money and
without price. —Isaiah 55:1

Until we meet Christ, we are all thirsty for something we
can't quite identify. We sample first one well and then
another to slake our powerful thirst. The well of human
wisdom offers potions to impart meaning to our existence,
the fountain of human love extends a tonic to soothe
our emotions, and the spring of accomplishment boosts
our self-esteem. These may seem to be acceptable wells,
but they provide only temporary relief. We even drink

polluted water from broken wells of addiction, extensive entertainment, and inappropriate sexual behavior; these leave us dehydrated.

Prophecy Fulfilled

Jesus answered and said to her, "If you knew the gift of God, and who it is who says to you, 'Give Me a drink,' you would have asked Him, and He would have given you living water." The woman said to Him, "Sir, You have nothing to draw with, and the well is deep. Where then do You get that living water? Are You greater than our father Jacob, who gave us the well, and drank from it himself, as well as his sons and his livestock?" Jesus answered and said to her, "Whoever drinks of this water will thirst again, but whoever drinks of the water that I shall give him will never thirst. But the water that I shall give him will become in him a fountain of water springing up into everlasting life." —John 4:10-14

He who believes in Me, as the Scripture has said, out of his heart will flow rivers of living water." —John 7:38

The woman at the well was completely depleted when she met Jesus; ironically, she offered *Him* water. He countered with the greatest offer of all time...the eternal thirst-quencher, Himself. Jesus promises to fill us and keep filling us. He also gives us the capacity to help water the arid land around us—as "rivers of living water" flow from our hearts, we act as divining rods, pointing the way for our friends and families, our country, and our world.

WRITING YOUR STORY

Experiencing drought? Beloved, the abundant life found in Jesus Christ should be our first drink every morning and our last sip before lights out! All day long let us drink from the "Deep, deep love of Jesus, vast, unmeasured, boundless, free, rolling as a mighty ocean, in its fullness over me" (Mark Ladd/Samuel T. Francis © Warner Chappell Music, Inc.).

Write down ideas for how you might make sure you stay spiritually hydrated.

DECEMBER 13

Jesus—Humble King

READING HIS STORY

Prophecy Proclaimed

"Rejoice greatly, O daughter of Zion! Shout, O daughter of Jerusalem! Behold, your King is coming to you; He is just and having salvation, lowly and riding on a donkey, a colt, the foal of a donkey. —Zechariah 9:9

Old Testament scholars looked at Zechariah 9 as evidence that the Messiah would come as a Divine warrior to render judgment against Israel's and to protect Jerusalem from harm Most were not expecting the humility expressed in verse 9. Though they understood Him as "just and having salvation," they missed His nature as "lowly and riding on a donkey."

Prophecy Fulfilled

Now when they drew near Jerusalem, and came to Bethphage, at the Mount of Olives, then Jesus sent two disciples, saying to them, "Go into the village opposite you, and immediately you will find a donkey tied, and a colt with her. Loose them and bring them to Me." ...All this was done that it might be fulfilled which was spoken by the prophet. —Matthew 21:1-2, 4

So the disciples went and did as Jesus commanded them. They brought the donkey and the colt, laid their clothes on them, and set Him on them. And a very great multitude spread their clothes on the road; others cut down branches from the trees and spread them on the road. Then the multitudes who went before and those who followed cried out, saying: "Hosanna to the Son of David! 'Blessed is He who comes in the name of the LORD!' Hosanna in the highest!" —Matthew 21:6-9

Now as He drew near, He saw the city and wept over it, saying, "If you had known, even you, especially in this your day, the things that make for your peace! But now they are hidden from your eyes. For days will come upon you when your enemies will build an embankment around you, surround you and close you in on every side, and level you, and your children within you, to the ground; and they will not leave in you one stone upon another, because you did not know the time of your visitation." —Luke 19:41-44

During Jesus' triumphal entry on Palm Sunday, we see Zechariah's prophecy fulfilled; simultaneously, Jesus, humbly and with tears, prophesies another event. Jerusalem will be leveled, He says, by enemies who "will not leave in you one stone upon another, because you did not know the time of your visitation." Most Bible scholars agree Jesus was speaking of what historians call the Siege of Jerusalem in 70 AD in which the Roman army captured the city of Jerusalem and destroyed both the city and its Temple.

WRITING YOUR STORY

Have you considered today as the "time of your visitation?" Jesus is a gentleman. He humbly invites you to know Him; He also weeps if you reject "the things that make for your peace." What will you do to draw closer to Him?

DECEMBER 14

Jesus—Man of Sorrows

READING HIS STORY

Prophecy Proclaimed

Then I said to them, "If it is agreeable to you, give me my wages; and if not, refrain." So they weighed out for my wages thirty pieces of silver. And the LORD said to me, "Throw it to the potter"—that princely price they set on me. So I took the thirty pieces of silver and threw them into the house of the LORD for the potter. —Zechariah 11:12-13

God uses the prophet Zechariah here to pronounce judgment (some 500 years before Jesus Christ) because the people of that day had rejected Zechariah and, by extension, the Lord Himself, as their shepherd. At the same time, the prophet points us to a future day—notice that Zechariah is directed to take the thirty pieces of silver and *throw* them into the house of the LORD for the potter.

Prophecy Fulfilled

Then one of the twelve, called Judas Iscariot, went to the chief priests and said, "What are you willing to give me if I deliver Him to you?" And they counted out to him thirty pieces of silver. So from that time he sought opportunity to betray Him. —Matthew 26:14-16

Then Judas, His betrayer, seeing that He had been condemned, was remorseful and brought back the thirty pieces of silver to the chief priests and elders, saying, "I have sinned by betraying innocent blood." And they said, "What is that to us? You see to it!" Then he threw down the pieces of silver in the temple and departed, and went and hanged himself. But the chief priests took the silver pieces and said, "It is not lawful to put them into the treasury, because they are the price of blood." And they consulted together and bought with them the potter's field, to bury strangers in. ...Then was fulfilled what was spoken by Jeremiah the prophet, saying, "And they took the thirty pieces of silver, the value of Him who was priced, whom they of the children of Israel priced, and gave them for the potter's field, as the LORD directed me." —Matthew 27:3-7, 9-10

Jesus had been Judas' shepherd for three close years— guiding, providing, sustaining, and walking beside him. Jesus had treated this man with the same love He showed to all of His disciples; He washed Judas' feet and sent those feet away in haste toward their appointed treachery saying, "What you do, do quickly." How the Lord's heart must have broken in that moment. After betraying Jesus, Judas, with remorse but without repentance, "threw down the pieces of silver in the temple." The Chief Priests "bought with them the potter's field" as a burial place for strangers.

WRITING YOUR STORY

No one knows the pain of betrayal better than Jesus, yet He looked on His lost disciple with love, sharing with him a last morsel of bread and a last opportunity to change directions. Have you a betrayer you need to forgive? Have you a course you need to amend?

DECEMBER 15

Jesus—Silent Sacrifice

READING HIS STORY

Prophecy Proclaimed

He was oppressed and He was afflicted, yet He opened not His mouth; He was led as a lamb to the slaughter, and as a sheep before its shearers is silent, so He opened not His mouth. —Isaiah 53:7

Jesus stood before the Sanhedrin, Pilate, the soldiers, and the people guiltless and, to their dismay, silent. He was beaten, mocked, maligned, disgraced, disfigured, and sentenced, yet he said nothing in His own defense. Why the silence?

Prophecy Fulfilled

Therefore My Father loves Me, because I lay down My life that I may take it again. No one takes it from Me, but I lay it down of Myself. I have power to lay it down, and I have power to take it again. This command I have received from My Father." —John 10:17-18

Pilate therefore said to Him, "Are You a king then?" Jesus answered, "You say rightly that I am a king. For this cause I was born, and for this cause I have come into the world, that I should bear witness to the truth. Everyone who is of the truth hears My voice." Pilate said to Him, "What is truth?" And when he had said this, he went out again to the Jews, and said to them, "I find no fault in Him at all." —John 18:37-38

Pilate stood before the Truth and knew the truth. While Jesus staggered under the weight of the cross, Pilate staggered under the weight of his own guilt. "I find no fault in Him," Pilate said, washing his hands in vain. And so Truth was crucified. Innocence was executed. The demons must have danced that day; little did they know, Jesus' silence would silence them!

WRITING YOUR STORY

Let's be silent before Jesus Christ, the Truth, sacrificing our need to explain ourselves or prop ourselves up. Let's let Him tell us where we need to repent and what crosses we need to bear. What is He telling you today?

DECEMBER 16

Jesus—Reviled & Robbed

READING HIS STORY

Prophecy Proclaimed

My God, My God, why have You forsaken Me? Why are You so far from helping Me, and from the words of My groaning?...But I am a worm, and no man; a reproach of men, and despised by the people. All those who see Me ridicule Me; they shoot out the lip, they shake the head saying, "He trusted in the Lord, let Him rescue Him; let Him deliver Him, since He delights in Him!"...The congregation of the wicked has enclosed Me. They pierced My hands and My feet; I can count all My bones. They look and stare at Me. They divide My garments among them, and for My clothing they cast lots. —Psalm 22:1, 6-8, 16-18

Psalm 22 provides a graphic prophecy of the Messiah's death on a cross. Most scholars date the Psalm to about a thousand years before the birth of Jesus. Crucifixion was originated by the Persians 400 years *after* the Psalm was written, in the sixth century BC; the Phoenicians introduced crucifixion to Rome in the third century BC, 700 years *after* the Psalm was written.

Prophecy Fulfilled

And those who passed by blasphemed Him, wagging their heads and saying, "You who destroy the temple and build it in three days, save Yourself! If You are the Son of God, come down from the cross." Likewise the chief priests also, mocking with the scribes and elders, said, "He saved others; Himself He cannot save. ...He trusted in God; let Him deliver Him now if He will have Him; for He said, 'I am the Son of God.' " —Matthew 27:39-43

Then the soldiers, when they had crucified Jesus, took His garments and made four parts, to each soldier a part, and also the tunic. Now the tunic was without seam, woven from the top in one piece. They said therefore among themselves, "Let us not tear it, but cast lots for it, whose it shall be,"

that the Scripture might be fulfilled which says:
"They divided My garments among them, and for
My clothing they cast lots." —John 19:23-24

Here we see our first-century contemporaries walking by
the cross, reviling Him and "wagging their heads." Can't you
just see a 21st-century crowd doing the same? The first-
century soldiers "cast lots" (gambled) for Jesus' clothing.
Even the finest details of Jesus' last moments fulfilled
prophecies regarding the Messiah.

WRITING YOUR STORY

Did cynicism crucify Christ? Hebrews 3:12 says, "Beware,
brethren, lest there be in any of you an evil heart of
unbelief." Ask the Lord to deliver you from cynicism and
soften your heart for His use.

DECEMBER 17

Jesus—Passover Lamb, Revisited

READING HIS STORY

Prophecy Proclaimed

Now the blood shall be a sign for you on the houses where you are. And when I see the blood, I will pass over you; and the plague shall not be on you to destroy you when I strike the land of Egypt. —Exodus 12:13

For seven days no leaven shall be found in your houses, since whoever eats what is leavened, that same person shall be cut off from the congregation of Israel, whether he is a stranger or a native of the land. —Exodus 12:19

"Behold, the days are coming," says the LORD, "That I will raise to David a Branch of righteousness; a King shall reign and prosper, and execute judgment and righteousness in the earth. In His days Judah will be saved, and Israel will dwell safely; now this is His name by which He will be called: THE LORD OUR RIGHTEOUSNESS." —Jeremiah 23:5-6

We discussed in this study on December 4 that Passover lambs were bred and nurtured in Bethlehem, Jesus' birthplace. Such lambs were considered perfect, symbolic of righteousness before God. Even then, only the best of the best made the five-and-a-half-mile trip to Jerusalem for Passover, the oldest and most important religious festival in Judaism.

Prophecy Fulfilled

And He said to them, "This is My blood of the new covenant, which is shed for many." —Mark 14:24

Likewise He also took the cup after supper, saying, "This cup is the new covenant in My blood, which is shed for you. —Luke 22:20

For He made Him who knew no sin to be sin for us, that we might become the righteousness of God in Him. —2 Corinthians 5:21

It's Passover week. Jesus enters Jerusalem through the Eastern Gate; the Passover lambs enter through the Sheep Gate. Jesus cleanses the temple; the Jewish people cleanse their homes of leaven (yeast), a symbol of sin. Jesus introduces the cup of "the new covenant in My blood, which is shed for you;" the Jewish people celebrate the Seder meal—retelling the story of the blood on the doorposts. They will miss the deeper meaning, spiritual redemption through the Messiah. Jesus is examined before Pilate; the Passover lambs are scrutinized. Jesus walks to Calvary; the priests sharpen their knives. Jesus commits His spirit to the Father; the Passover lambs lift their chins to the priests.

WRITING YOUR STORY

Christmas is our oldest and most important religious festival. As we mark our traditions, let's make sure we don't miss the deeper meaning. Write down your plan for focusing your heart and your home on Jesus.

DECEMBER 18

Jesus—Christ Alone

READING HIS STORY

Prophecy Proclaimed

You are of purer eyes than to behold evil, and cannot look on wickedness. —Habakkuk 1:13

"Awake, O sword, against My Shepherd, against the Man who is My Companion," says the LORD of hosts. "Strike the Shepherd, and the sheep will be scattered..." —Zechariah 13:7

Jesus was completely isolated when He went to the cross. After an evening of fellowship during the Passover meal, Jesus' disciples progressively abandoned him. They failed to "watch and pray" in the Garden of Gethsemane, leaving Jesus to wrestle alone with the temptation to "let this cup pass." At His arrest, the disciples departed and denied. Even those at the foot of the cross hopelessly mourned not only His death but also their own loss of hope. Jesus alone remained faithful; He alone accomplished salvation. Finally, even the Father, with "purer eyes than to behold evil," turned His face from Jesus.

Prophecy Fulfilled

Then Jesus said to them, "All of you will be [a] made to stumble because of Me this night, for it is written: 'I will strike the Shepherd, and the sheep of the flock will be scattered.'" —Matthew 26:31

But all this was done that the Scriptures of the prophets might be fulfilled. Then all the disciples forsook Him and fled. —Matthew 26:56

And about the ninth hour Jesus cried out with a loud voice, saying, "Eli, Eli, lama sabachthani?" that is, "My God, My God, why have You forsaken Me?" —Matthew 27:46

While David could proclaim in Psalm 23, "though I walk through the valley of the shadow of death, I will fear no evil; for You are with me," Jesus claimed no such blessing, crying out instead, "My God, My God, why have You forsaken Me?" This was a rhetorical question; Jesus knew why His father could not look at Him—He who knew no sin had become sin "that we might become the righteousness of God" (2 Corinthians 5:21).

WRITING YOUR STORY

Believer, you do not have to face this world, or the transition to the next, alone. Seeker, Jesus desires your fellowship. He has promised to be with His own "always, even to the end of the age" (Matthew 28:20). Thank Him for His sustaining presence.

DECEMBER 19

Jesus—Our Healer

READING HIS STORY

Prophecy Proclaimed

For dogs have surrounded Me; the congregation of the wicked has enclosed Me. They pierced My hands and My feet. —Psalm 22:16

Surely He has borne our griefs and carried our sorrows; yet we esteemed Him stricken, smitten by God, and afflicted. But He was wounded for our transgressions, He was bruised for our iniquities; the chastisement for our peace was upon Him, and by His stripes we are healed. All we like sheep have gone astray; we have turned, every one, to his own way; and the LORD has laid on Him the iniquity of us all. —Isaiah 53:4-6

The name Isaiah literally means "Salvation of God" or "God Saves." Isaiah is both prophet and evangelist. Though he is foretelling the future (he is writing about 800 years before Jesus' birth), he describes the events of Christ's death vividly as if writing about the past—calling us to respond to the Savior King. "He was wounded for our transgressions," Isaiah pleads, "bruised for our iniquities... And by His stripes we are healed." Read all of Psalm 22 and Isaiah 53 and consider all of the prophetic treasure in these passages. Isaiah, along with the Psalmist, paint a highly specific picture of crucifixion before such punishment exists. What do Jesus' stripes heal us from? We are healed from sin—both the burden it adds to our lives on Earth and the punishment it brings forever in Hell.

Prophecy Fulfilled

> But one of the soldiers pierced His side with a spear, and immediately blood and water came out. —John 19:34

The blood and water show us two important aspects of the Lord's death: redemption (blood) and a fountain of spiritual life (water). Because Jesus shed His blood to redeem us, we can be forgiven and cleansed of all our sins. Our redemption is for a purpose: God wants us to live in Christ.

This is possible because of the life-imparting aspect of Jesus' death.

Sadly, the amazing prophetic story in Psalm 22 and Isaiah 53 and the fulfillment recorded in the New Testament continue to be ignored by people who hold to a dogma against the miracle of prophecy, refusing to accept that a God who created time itself knows the future.

WRITING YOUR STORY

Jesus was pierced for all transgressions for all time. Every sin ever committed hung on the cross with Him. Have you laid your burden at His nail-pierced feet? Do so today, and the prophecy for your life is peace now and forever. List any burdens you still must lay down.

DECEMBER 20

Jesus—Our Wholeness

READING HIS STORY

Prophecy Proclaimed

He guards all his bones; not one of them is broken.
—Psalm 34:20

And I will pour on the house of David and on the inhabitants of Jerusalem the Spirit of grace and supplication; then they will look on Me whom they pierced. Yes, they will mourn for Him as one mourns for his only son. —Zechariah 12:10

Crucifixion was one of the most agonizing forms of capital punishment in history. Though it could be accomplished quickly by suspending the arms above the head, the method for Jesus involved stretching the arms parallel and nailing them to a horizontal bar. To speed death, executioners would often break victims' legs; with legs broken, those crucified could no longer use their thigh muscles to push their weight up and breathe. This was the plan for Jesus and the two thieves beside Him, specifically because the Jewish leaders wanted the three bodies removed before the Sabbath.

Prophecy Fulfilled

Therefore, because it was the Preparation Day, that the bodies should not remain on the cross on the Sabbath (for that Sabbath was a high day), the Jews asked Pilate that their legs might be broken, and that they might be taken away. Then the soldiers came and broke the legs of the first and of the other who was crucified with Him. But when they came to Jesus and saw that He was already dead, they did not break His legs. But one of the soldiers pierced His side with a spear, and immediately blood and water came out. And he who has seen has testified, and his testimony is true; and he knows that he is telling the truth, so that you may believe. For these things were done that the Scripture should be fulfilled, "Not one of His bones shall be broken." And again another

Scripture says, "They shall look on Him whom they pierced." —John 19:31-37

Why dwell on the grizzly details? While the legs of the thieves were broken, Jesus' bones were left whole to fulfill prophecy. The blood and water that poured from His pierced side evidenced pericardial fluid around the heart. He did not die because of broken bones; Jesus quite literally died of a broken heart.

WRITING YOUR STORY

Sin fragments our lives and clouds our futures; as we confess our brokenness, Jesus makes us whole. Use this space today to discuss with Jesus your need for spiritual healing.

DECEMBER 21

Jesus—Buried With the Rich

READING HIS STORY

Prophecy Proclaimed

And they made His grave with the wicked—but
with the rich at His death, because He had done
no violence, nor was any deceit in His mouth.
—Isaiah 53:9

As a condemned, so-called criminal with no home, no
earthly goods, nothing but the clothes on His back—and
those having been gambled for and taken—Jesus was
scheduled to have made "His grave with the wicked." His
body might have been buried in an unmarked grave in a
place of shame, but that's not what the prophet foretold in
the Messianic chapter we already studied on December 19

in the Book of Isaiah. It's also not something Jesus' disciple, Joseph of Arimathea, would stand for.

Prophecy Fulfilled

> Now when evening had come, there came a rich man from Arimathea, named Joseph, who himself had also become a disciple of Jesus. This man went to Pilate and asked for the body of Jesus. Then Pilate commanded the body to be given to him. When Joseph had taken the body, he wrapped it in a clean linen cloth, and laid it in his new tomb which he had hewn out of the rock; and he rolled a large stone against the door of the tomb, and departed. —Matthew 27:57-60

Joseph, a rich man, lovingly removed Jesus' body from the cross, wrapped it in linen, and laid it in his own new rock-hewn tomb outside the city. According to a *National Geographic* report, a team of researchers from the National Technical University of Athens carefully inspected in 2016 a site long marked as the burial site of Jesus Christ and found "evidence to suggest that the identification of the site by representatives of the Roman emperor Constantine may be a reasonable one." *National Geographic's* archeologist-in-residence, Fredrik Hiebert, said at the time, "My knees are shaking a little bit because I wasn't expecting this....

It appears to be visible proof that the location of the tomb has not shifted through time, something that scientists and historians have wondered for decades."

WRITING YOUR STORY

Whether or not the *National Geographic* story proves accurate, we can say for certain that the Word of God does not shift over time. Every prophecy has been or will be fulfilled. Every promise has been or will be delivered by our God. Thank Him for His faithfulness in your life.

DECEMBER 22

Jesus—The Risen One

READING HIS STORY

Prophecy Proclaimed

Therefore my heart is glad, and my glory rejoices; my flesh also will rest in hope. For You will not leave my soul in Sheol, nor will You allow Your Holy One to see corruption. —Psalm 16:9-10

For I know that my Redeemer lives, and He shall stand at last on the earth; and after my skin is destroyed, this I know, that in my flesh I shall see God, Whom I shall see for myself, and my eyes shall behold, and not another. How my heart yearns within me! —Job 19:25-27

David counted his own soul as eternally safe because the Messiah, God's Holy One, would rise again. His flesh could "rest in hope." Job also trusted in Christ's resurrection, and in his own. These saints believed the resurrection before it happened! How much more should we who have the evidence before us place our hope in the Risen One?

Prophecy Fulfilled

> And behold, there was a great earthquake; for an angel of the Lord descended from heaven, and came and rolled back the stone from the door, and sat on it. His countenance was like lightning, and his clothing as white as snow. And the guards shook for fear of him, and became like dead men. But the angel answered and said to the women, "Do not be afraid, for I know that you seek Jesus who was crucified. He is not here; for He is risen, as He said. Come, see the place where the Lord lay. And go quickly and tell His disciples that He is risen from the dead, and indeed He is going before you into Galilee; there you will see Him. Behold, I have told you." —Matthew 28:2-7

The evidence is overwhelming. Consider just a few facts. Jesus' disciples, who ran away like frightened children when He was arrested, became fearless Gospel messengers after the resurrection. They chose to die as martyrs rather than recant their undeniable experience! No body was ever found—if one had been available, either the Jewish or Roman authorities (both loathed the preaching of the resurrection) certainly would have brought it forward. And since, as Paul tells us, some 500 eyewitnesses who saw the Risen Christ were still alive in 56 AD (see 1 Corinthians 15:3-8), even the most skilled liars could not have convinced first-century dwellers the resurrection was anything but true.

WRITING YOUR STORY

Paul tells us, "If Christ is not risen, then our preaching is empty and your faith is also empty" (1 Corinthians 15:14). If, however, He is alive—as David and Job believed beforehand and as Jesus' disciples confirmed—He has defeated death. He is King Eternal. And we owe Him our allegiance. Where do you stand?

DECEMBER 23

Jesus—Our Traveling Companion

READING HIS STORY

Prophecy Proclaimed

Now behold, two of them were traveling that same day to a village called Emmaus, which was seven miles from Jerusalem. And they talked together of all these things which had happened. So it was, while they conversed and reasoned, that Jesus Himself drew near and went with them. ...Then He said to them, "O foolish ones, and slow of heart to believe in all that the prophets have spoken! Ought not the Christ to have suffered these things and to enter into His glory?" And beginning

> at Moses and all the Prophets, He expounded to
> them in all the Scriptures the things concerning
> Himself. ...And they said to one another, "Did not
> our heart burn within us while He talked with us
> on the road, and while He opened the Scriptures
> to us?" —Luke 24:13-15, 25-26, 32

In this astonishing passage, Jesus takes two unnamed disciples on a prophetic journey within a journey. The disciples are traveling on a physical road to a town called Emmaus and Jesus takes them spiritually from Point A of Blindness and Defeat to Point B of Illumination and Hope. "And beginning at Moses and all the Prophets, He expounded to them in all the Scriptures the things concerning Himself." We can only imagine how they must have felt. For a fuller understanding, read all of Luke 24:13-35.

Prophecy Fulfilled

> But when the Helper comes, whom I shall send
> to you from the Father, the Spirit of truth who
> proceeds from the Father, He will testify of Me.
> —John 15:26

We don't have to imagine how those early disciples felt! Jesus told us, "When the Helper comes, whom I shall send to you from the Father, the Spirit of Truth who proceeds from the Father, He will testify of Me." We "anonymous disciples" of the 21st Century have the same Traveling Companion on our road as did the two on their way to Emmaus. As we read Scripture, Jesus' prophecy about the Holy Spirit's work is fulfilled in our lives, for the Holy Spirit testifies of Jesus, bringing to our minds supernatural understanding and direction.

WRITING YOUR STORY

Have you met Jesus on your road? Have you surrendered your life and received the Holy Spirit? Are you walking with Him? If so, write about what you have learned on your journey. If you have not yet established a relationship with the Friend who sticks "closer than a brother" (see Proverbs 18:24), what's stopping you?

DECEMBER 24

Jesus—The Ascended One

READING HIS STORY

Prophecy Proclaimed

You have ascended on high, You have led captivity captive; You have received gifts among men, even from the rebellious, that the LORD God might dwell there. —Psalm 68:18

Through His finished work on the cross, Jesus literally took sin as His prisoner for all time. During this beautiful Christmas season, we have beheld Him as a babe in Mary's arms, looked Him in the eyes as a friend who walks alongside us, and seen Him through tears as the silent suffering servant on Calvary's cross. Let's take a wide-eyed look at Him today as the conquering warrior who defeated death, "led captivity captive," and, victorious evermore, ascended on high.

Prophecy Fulfilled

So then, after the Lord had spoken to them, He was received up into heaven, and sat down at the right hand of God. —Mark 16:19

Here are two things to ponder today about Jesus' position at God's right hand. 1) Ephesians 1:20-21 says that this position is, "...far above all principality and power and might and dominion, and every name that is named, not only in this age but also in that which is to come." 2) Romans 8:34 teaches, "Who is he who condemns? It is Christ who died, and furthermore is also risen, who is even at the right hand of God, who also makes intercession for us."

WRITING YOUR STORY

Jesus Christ is the greatest authority of all time. Though He has every right to do so, He does not condemn His sin-ridden subjects. In fact, as believers face the difficulties of this life, He is actually praying for us. Could we have a more powerful prayer warrior than the Ascended One?

DECEMBER 25

Jesus—Soon-Coming King

READING HIS STORY

Prophecy Proclaimed

> Of the increase of His government and peace there will be no end, upon the throne of David and over His kingdom, to order it and establish it with judgment and justice from that time forward, even forever. The zeal of the LORD of hosts will perform this. —Isaiah 9:7

The word "advent" means "coming" or "arrival." We have been studying the life of Jesus for the month of December in preparation for the celebration of Jesus' first advent in Bethlehem. It is also a time to celebrate anew the advent of Jesus as Savior in our own lives and to anticipate His coming again. The fact is Christ has come. He is present in the world today. And He will come again in power.

Prophecy Fulfilled

Now I saw heaven opened, and behold, a white horse. And He who sat on him was called Faithful and True, and in righteousness He judges and makes war. His eyes were like a flame of fire, and on His head were many crowns. He had a name written that no one knew except Himself. He was clothed with a robe dipped in blood, and His name is called The Word of God. And the armies in heaven, clothed in fine linen, white and clean, followed Him on white horses. Now out of His mouth goes a sharp sword, that with it He should strike the nations. And He Himself will rule them with a rod of iron. He Himself treads the winepress of the fierceness and wrath of Almighty God. And He has on His robe and on His thigh a name written: KING OF KINGS AND LORD OF LORDS. —Revelation 19:11-16

This passage should leave us breathless. Despite all the challenges we have faced this year—and in every other difficult year—when Jesus comes again, He will right every wrong. As Isaiah said, "Of the increase of His government and peace, there will be no end." We do not know the day or the hour, but we can be certain that this prophecy, too, shall be fulfilled—perhaps in only a moment.

WRITING YOUR STORY

Those who know the Lord Jesus Christ as their Soon-Coming King have a privileged identity and unshakable confidence in this life and are forever safe in His realm. Where is your hope for the coming New Year? For the next decade? For eternity?

DISCOVER JESUS

It's been our pleasure to bring you this mini Bible study, "25 Days of Anticipation" from Love Worth Finding.

If you're still unsure about your personal relationship with Jesus Christ, we invite you to listen to some messages from Adrian Rogers. We think you'll find both comfort and hope in Pastor Rogers' simply stated explanation of the Gospel. **Go to: lwf.org/discover-jesus**

CENTER FOR BIBLICAL LEARNING

GET STARTED

Perhaps you're a new Christian. If so, welcome to the family! One of the best ways to get started in your new faith walk is to complete the series *What Every Christian Ought to Know* from Pastor Adrian Rogers. This can be completed as an individual, in a one-on-one mentoring format, or in a small group. All three studies are available in our Biblical Learning Center. **Go to: lwf.org/biblical-learning-center**

WHY LOVE WORTH FINDING?

If you've been with Love Worth Finding for some time, you know that our heart is to bring people to Jesus Christ and mature them in the faith. Maybe God is calling you to support that mission. Find out how to partner with us. **Go to: lwf.org/why-lwf**

Again, thanks so much for joining us in this advent study. Be sure and check back with us soon at **lwf.org or on the MyLWF App** for more encouragement from Love Worth Finding.